THE COMPANIONSHIP OF THE HOLY SPIRIT

*No, I will not abandon you as orphans—
I will come to you.*
John 14:18 *NLT*

The Companionship of the Holy Spirit

Copyright 2016 by Franklin N. Abazie

ISBN 978-1-945133-00-8

All rights reserved. This book or any portion thereof may not be reproduced or used in any manner whatsoever without the express written permission of the publisher, except for the use of brief quotations in a book review. All Bible quotes are from King James Version and others as noted.

Published by: **F N ABAZIE PUBLISHING HOUSE –**
aka Empowerment Bookstore.

Psalms 26:7
That I may publish with the voice of thanksgiving and tell of all thy wondrous works.

To order additional copies, wholesales or booking:
Call the Church office 973-372-7518, or
call Empowerment Bookstore Hotline 973-393-8518

Worship address:
343 Sanford Avenue Newark New Jersey 07106
Administrative Head Office address:
33 Schley Street Newark New Jersey 07112
Email:pastoprfranknto@yahoo.com
Website www.fnabaziehealingministries.org
Coming soon www.fnabaziepublishinghouse.org

This book is a production of F N Abazie Publishing House.
A publication Arms of Miracle of God Ministries 2016 First Edition

CONTENTS

THE MANDATE OF THE COMMISSION.................... iv

INTRODUCTION... vii

CHAPTER 1
WHO IS THE HOLY SPIRIT?................................ 1

CHAPTER 2
THE WORKS & OPERATION OF THE HOLY SPIRIT..... 15

CHAPTER 3
THE GUIDANCE & ACQUAINTANCE OF THE HOLY SPIRIT 25

CHAPTER 4
ENJOYING THE LEADERSHIP OF THE HOLY SPIRIT... 30

CHAPTER 5
OVERCOMING TRIALS BY THE HELP OF THE HOLY SPIRIT 49

MIRACLE CARE OUTREACH................................ 75

MIRACLE OF GOD MINISTRIES 78

ABOUT THE AUTHOR.. 82

BOOKS BY REV FRANKLIN N. ABAZIE 84

THE MANDATE OF THE COMMISSION

"THE MOMENT IS DUE TO IMPACT YOUR WORLD THROUGH THE REVIVAL OF THE HEALING & MIRACLE MINISTRY OF JESUS CHRIST OF NAZARETH. I AM SENDING YOU TO RESTORE HEALTH UNTO THEE AND I WILL HEAL THEE OF THY WOUNDS. SAID THE LORD OF HOST"

ARMS OF THE COMMISSION

1) F N Abazie Ministries-Miracle of God Ministries (Miracle Chapel Intl.)

2) F N Abazie TV Ministries: Global Television Ministry Outreach.

3) F N Abazie Radio Ministries: Radio Broadcasting Outreach.

4) F N Abazie Publishing House: Book Publication.

5) F N Abazie Bible School: also called Word of Healing Bible School (W.O.H.B.S)

6) F N Abazie Evangelistic Ass: Miracle of God Ministries: Global Crusade

7) Empowerment Bookstore: Book distribution.

8) F N Abazie Helping Hands: Meeting the help of the needy world wide

9) F N Abazie Disaster Recovery Mission: Global Disaster Recovery.

10) F N Abazie Prison Ministry: Prison Ministry for all convicts "Second chance

> Some of our ministry arms are waiting the appointed time to commence.

INTRODUCTION

Although I may say one or more words subsequently, but I found one outstanding scripture that summarizes my introduction page of this book: THE COMPANIONSHIP OF THE HOLY SPIRIT

Now the Lord is that Spirit: and where the Spirit of the Lord is, there is liberty.
2 Cor. 3:17

That is my introduction in a nutshell.

John 14:26

But when the Father sends the Advocate as my representative—that is, the Holy Spirit—he will teach you everything and will remind you of everything I have told you.

Although we live in a dispensation of the Holy Spirit, the Holy Spirit has been grieved and hurt by millions of Christians. You may ask how? By mere NEGLECT & IGNORANCE of the person of the Holy Spirit. Before I go further realize with me that the Holy Spirit is God the trinity, He is a person. He speaks, feels, touches, taste and hear. Contrary to our limited understanding of Him, He is a person. The Holy Spirit is not a thing or an object. So then because He is a person, therefore He has emotions, he thinks, he has a mind, he can be grieved and He can be happy.

Ephesians 4:31 *NLT*

And do not bring sorrow to God's Holy Spirit by the way you live. Remember, he has identified you as his own, guaranteeing that you will be saved on the day of redemption.

Acknowledge therefore that the Holy Spirit is God, He is an advocate and a representative of the supreme sovereign power of God. As a caretaker and representative, He is interested in all you do as a person.

Acts 17:20

For in him we live, and move, and have our being; as certain also of your own poets have said, For we are also his offspring.

Holm Christian standard Bible puts it this way.

Phils. 2:13

For it is God who is working in you, enabling you both to desire and to work out His good purpose.

There is nothing we (believers, non-believers) can achieve and innovate in this race of life without the help of the Holy Spirit. Consider that in the Old Testament the Holy Spirit is the Spirit of creation.

THE HOLY SPIRIT IS THE SPIRIT OF CREATION

Genesis 1:2-3

And the earth was without form, and void; and darkness was upon the face of the deep. And the Spirit of God moved upon the face of the waters. And God said, Let there be light: and there was light.

Without any contradiction, there is no substitute or I should use alternative to the Holy Spirit. If you have ever seen anything new in this modern age, it is by the creative forces of the Holy Spirit. Although most acclaimed scientist place more emphasizes on their intellectual knowledge. Accolades has been grossly misrepresented and misinterpreted. In my own opinion, everything you see and witness today from the social media, to Google, yahoo, online banking, Uber technology, man going to live in the belly of the ocean & inside the moon are all by the help of the Holy Spirit. Therefore acknowledge Him in your life, pray and ask him to do something new in your life. (See **Isaiah 43:18-19**).

THE HOLY SPIRIT IS THE REVEALER OF SECRETS.

John 16:13

Howbeit when he, the Spirit of truth, is come, he will guide you into all truth: for he shall not speak of himself; but whatsoever he shall hear, that shall he speak: and he will shew you things to come

Remember the secret things belongs unto God… Until the Holy Spirit reveals it to you, it remains Gods secret.

Deuteronomy 29:29 *The secret things belongs to the Lord our God, but the things revealed belong to us and to our children forever, that we may follow all the words of this law.*

The Holy Spirit is a revealer of the deep things of God, He searches and reveals the deep things of God. He has a powerful mind, full with the infinite manifold wisdom of God.

THE HOLY SPIRIT MAKES INTERCESSION FOR US BEFORE THE FATHER

Romans 8:26

Likewise the Spirit also helpeth our infirmities: for we know not what we should pray for as we ought: but the Spirit itself maketh intercession for us with groanings which cannot be uttered.

THE HOLY SPIRIT IS OUR TEACHER

1 Cor. 2:13

Which things also we speak, not in the words which man's wisdom teacheth, but which the Holy Ghost teacheth…

As a student of the Holy Spirit allow the Holy Spirit to teach you more in this book, the things you need to know and the techniques to draw near to the Holy Spirit. In these dreadful days we cannot do without the companionship of the Holy Spirit. Understand what we are saying. We live in the age were all struggles of life, and challenges of life are based on faith, and ones believe system. The Muslim and ISIS have taken their Jihad to our churches, and corridors. Rumors and threats of terrorism have risen beyond our human imagination. It is high time we introduce the person of the Holy Spirit to the scene. As our very present help in times of trouble He will avenge for us against the adversaries.

Although you may all not agree with me, but I am persuaded to say this, almost all of your life challenges has a spiritual root. All the hindrances, obstacles and attacks that has prevailed in your life, is deeply rooted in the realms of the SPIRIT.

Ephesians 6:12

For we wrestle not against flesh and blood, but against principalities, against powers, against the rulers of the darkness of this world, against spiritual wickedness in high places.

In these last days, forces of evil have been released on a higher scale. These forces have power to intimidate, dominate and manipulate the lives and destinies of the believer. The believer must also provoke the Holy Spirit and the Host of Angels to appear on the scene for this end time struggle. In these last days the devil is at loose in numerous systematic dimensions. Threatening news of terror, fear and calamity is everywhere. It is time we introduce the Holy Spirit to the scene.

Allow me to make this strong statement out of faith:
"SPIRITUAL battles are higher than PHYSICAL battles" With these lines in mind, until you overcome the enemy in the realms of the SPIRIT the prevailing challenges has power to prevail. You will agree with me that at one point in your life journey, prevailing challenges dominated and remote controlled your life. It is my desire in this book that you turn to the Holy Spirit.

Come with me as we call down supreme forces of Heaven by the help of the Holy Spirit to super-impose divine and heaven verdict concerning the welfare, life and destiny of the believer.

Happy reading.

Highlights

HOW TO RECEIVE THE HOLY SPIRIT

1) REPENT: Peter replied to a question from the crowd "what shall we do?" *"Repent and be baptized every one of you, in the name of Jesus Christ for the forgiveness of your sins. And you will receive the gift of the Holy Spirit"* **Acts 2:38**. It is easy for the Holy Spirit to use any humble soul. *For a broken Spirit; a broken and a contrite heart, O God, you will not despise.* **Psalms 51:17** genuine repentance is the key and the only access to receive & activate the presence of the Holy Spirit.

2) FAITH: **Jude 1:20** *But ye beloved, building up your selves on your most holy faith, praying in the Holy Ghost.* Most prevailing sinful habits, hinders and grieves the Holy Spirit in your life. Unless you develop strong faith, those sinful habits have power to prevail. **Romans 6:14** ... *Sin shall not have dominion over me.* The faith we are talking here is your ability to make a decision for Jesus Christ. Therefore develop faith that will crush all prevailing remote control forces. I see your faith bring you deliverance over that prevailing lustful situation. Do

you enjoy His presence? Therefore allow the Holy Spirit to become your companion.

3) DECISION: Decision is the entrance door in to his presence. Although the Holy Spirit has been working through and in you. The manifestation of His manifold presence has been waiting for you to make a decision. Have you decided to accept the person of the Holy Spirit? Until you repent and accept Jesus Christ as your Lord and savior you are not ready to receive the Holy Spirit. All forces in hell know when you make up your mind. In 2006 I found myself in a difficult challenge of my life that it took faith and a decision in 2008 to overcome it. In your life time decisions are vital keys to remain in the flight of success & excellence. Decisions are the pillars to determine the outcome of your life. Most of the things that happened in your lifetime are a function of decision. Decisions are the gateway into your freedom, liberty and a glorious future. When you settle for less, you can only get what is entitled for the less privilege. (See **Luke 16:21**.) Despite all the riches of the father, the prodigal son took a drastic decision that reduced him to eat the pig's food, until he came to himself.... **Luke 15:17** Although you might not have noticed nor considered these your

lifestyle is wrapped in the decision you make. All of these prevailing forces, that have molded your lifestyle did not happen overnight. At some point in your lifetime, you made a decision and invited certain controlling forces in your life. You are free until you decide to marry. King Solomon was right with God until he decided to go after strange women. **(1 Kings 11:1-6)**. David brought a sword into his family when he murdered Uriah the Hittite. Take a decision today and evict the old man of sin. (See **Romans 6:1-14**).

4) PRAYER: **Jude 1:20** *But ye beloved, building up your selves on your most holy faith, praying in the Holy Ghost.* The Bible says likewise the Spirit also helpeth our infirmities; for we know not what we should pray for as we ought: but the Spirit itself maketh intercession for us with groaning which cannot be uttered. Prayer is so vital in our lives, because anytime you pray in tongue you provoke the presence of the Holy Spirit. Most of the relief and assurance that will come in to your life is by the assistance of the Holy Spirit.

PRAYER POINT TO ACTIVATE THE PRESENCE OF THE HOLY SPIRIT

1) Holy Spirit reveal yourself to me in the Name of Jesus.

2) Holy Spirit crush every daily habit of sin in the Name of Jesus.

3) Holy Spirit become my companion today in the Name of Jesus.

4) Holy Spirit grant me access in the Name of Jesus.

5) Power of God, grant me the GRACE to live right for Jesus Christ.

6) Hand of God, deliver me from sin in the Name of Jesus.

7) Fire of God, burn every sinful thoughts from my mind in the Name of Jesus.

8) I proclaim authority over every prevailing sin in my life in Jesus Name.

9) I destroy every root of sin in my life in Jesus Name.

10) Sin shall not have dominion over my life in the Name of Jesus.

11) Lord God, Emphasize genuine repentance over my Spirit man in the Name of Jesus

12) Holy Spirit, revive & rekindle your fire of revival inside of me in the Name of Jesus.

13) Power of God hijack the controlling forces oppressing my life in the Name of Jesus.

14) Blood of Jesus take over my life in the Name of Jesus.

15) O Lord, baptize me with the gift of the Holy Spirit.

16) Holy Spirit breathe afresh upon my life in the Name of Jesus.

17) Holy Spirit take possession of my will in the Name of Jesus.

18) Holy Spirit make yourself real to me in the name of Jesus

19) Holy Spirit fan your revival fire upon my life in the name of Jesus

INTRODUCTION

CONGRATULATIONS

Appreciate the help and work of the Holy Spirit in your life. Never neglect nor ignore the presence of the Holy Spirit over the affairs of your life. No ma especially in the kingdom of God can go further without the help of the Holy Spirit over the affairs of their lives or ministry. The Holy Spirit is our very present help in time of trouble.

Just like the title, I see you developing an acquaintance and forming a companionship of the Holy Spirit. Make the Holy Spirit your senior partner in life today and enjoy a sweet ride over the obstacle and mountains of challenges of life.

I thank God for your life. Now that you have repeated these prayers out loud, enjoy and comprehend the companionship of the Holy Spirit. May the Holy Spirit breathe on you afresh as you read. Amen

CHAPTER 1

WHO IS THE HOLY SPIRIT?

Although Bible scholars has made remarkable references about Him, the Holy Spirit is God the trinity, he is a person with emotions just like you. He has a mind, thinks, loves, speaks, and hears, he can be grieved and wounded. In my own opinion the Holy Spirit is the Spirit of the Lord.

2 Cor. 3:17

Now the Lord is that Spirit: and where the Spirit of the Lord is, there is liberty. So many of us do not know that.

We live in a dispensation of the Holy Spirit that is why Jesus said nevertheless I tell you the truth; it is expedient for you that I go away: for if I go not away, the comforter will not come unto you; but if I depart, I will send him unto you. Although so many of us ignore and neglect him; we all as believer must acknowledge that, there is nothing we can accomplish in life without the help of the Holy Spirit.

John 14:26

But the comforter, which is the Holy Ghost, whom the Father will send in my name, he shall teach you all things, and bring all things to your remembrance, whatsoever I have said unto you.

The Holy Spirit as the comforter, Jesus himself needed him most, to strengthen him before his death. The Bible says how God anointed Jesus of Nazareth with Holy Ghost and with power; who went about doing good, and healing all who were oppressed of the devil; for God was with him.

The Holy Spirit is the comforter, Jesus said I will not leave you comfortless: I will come to you. (See **John 14:26**.) Hence, Jesus empowered his disciples when he finally came back shortly before his ascension into heaven.

John 20:22

And when he had said this, he breathed on them, and saith unto them "Receive ye the Holy Ghost"

Although the Holy Spirit is the spirit of creation, he is also the quickening Spirit, he reveals, directs, instructs and corrects. Despite the dwelling of the Holy Spirit in us the only forces that has power to hinder and repel the Holy Spirit is SIN. In this evil generation we live in sin has become the vogue of the day. The demand for Sin and the requirement for immoralities have crumbled the life of the moral man (born with a conscience). Man has left the biblical definition of marriage and has wandered into all forms and appearance of a lustful lifestyle. Although most of us will love to live a righteous lifestyle, the prevailing and dominating controlling forces of sin have forced almost everyone in this end time generation to accommodate the lifestyle of sin, at least to a degree.

Few days ago, someone was telling me how they are "heartbroken" because they broke up in their relationship. Without contradiction I thought they were in a man and woman relationship. Although I made a few comments, I was baffled and short of words when I discovered it was not the relationship I had in mind.

What is Sin? One may ask...

One man said S.I.N means Satan Identification Number, I do not disagree, but it is incomplete. In my own definition, sin is disobeying God words and commandments. Every time you operate outside of the commandment of God you are committing sin. **1 John 3:8** *He that committeth sin is of the devil; for the devil sinneth from the beginning. For this purpose the son of God was manifested that he might destroy the works of the devil.*

Proverbs 14:34

Sin is a reproach to any nation

Globally, without doubt, sin has prevailed in this immoral generation. The mind of humans has been greatly corrupted into evil and lustful behaviors .No matter how you define it, freedom of right, or animal rights , the common man has made another alternative for a best friend and a marriage/bedroom partners.

Proverbs 14:19

The evil bow before the good...

Despite what David said in **Psalms 51:3** For I acknowledge my transgressions and my sin is ever before me. We must not take the purpose of the coming, life and death of Jesus in vain. Man was nature was born in sin like David attested. **Psalms 51:5** *Behold I was shapen in iniquity; and in sin did my mother conceive me.*

Who is a Sinner?

There is a dominating controlling force that pushes us all into a sinful lifestyle. Until such forces are crushed, it has power to prevail over the life of the believer. In the subject of who is a sinner, there is no exemption, everyone is included. It's time to tell yourself the truth. Is there any hidden sinful lifestyle you are dealing with? Confess it and crush it in the open with prayers.

2 Cor. 13:5

Examine yourselves, whether ye be in the faith; prove your own selves. Know ye not your own selves, how that Jesus Christ is in you, except ye be reprobates?

Although most faith people live in denial about the work of the flesh, from my own scriptural understanding everyone operating within the scope of **Galatians 5:20-21** is classified as a sinner.

Gal. 5:20-21

Now the works of the flesh are manifest, which are these; Adultery, fornication, uncleanness, lasciviousness, Idolatry, witchcraft, hatred, variance, emulations, wrath, strife, seditions, heresies, envyings, murders, drunkenness, revellings, and such like: of the which I tell you before, as I have also told you in time past, that they which do such things shall not inherit the kingdom of God.

Further supporting scripture…

Rev. 21:8

But the fearful, and unbelieving, and the abominable, and murderers, and whoremongers, and sorcerers, and idolaters, and all liars, shall have their part in the lake which burneth with fire and brimstone: which is the second death.

Who is therefore a sinner?

1) The Lazy Man: It is sinful for any able bodied man/woman to fold their hand and make themselves beggars. The Bible says the sluggard will not plow by reason of the cold; therefore shall he beg in harvest, and have nothing. In my own understanding laziness is a sin. **2 Thess. 3:10** *For even when we were with you, this we commanded you, that if any would not work, neither should he eat.* Covenant mentality demands that we all understand that God has done His part over our lives. Jesus said I must work. It is dignity for every believer to earn money through the work of their hands. Although most lazy people live in denial, and tend to tend to use prayer and fasting to cover up, nevertheless, Godliness demands

that we take absolute responsibility on the outcome of our lives.

2) Unbelievers: In my own view all that have not acknowledged Jesus Christ as Lord and savior are sinners. The Bible says God heareth not sinners. Without contradiction all unbelievers live in a sinful lifestyle. Unless God has mercy most unbelievers will not make eternity in heaven.

3) Lies: All liars are sinners before the Almighty God. Lying is a very serious sin, simple because it leads to poverty and shame. Lying decays great destiny and erodes potential future. Someone that I know very well lies so much to themselves, that they became a beggar by paralyzing their future, and they frustrated the will of God over their life.

How do I come out of sin?

These prevailing dominating controlling forces will not casually go away. Unless you taking actions by faith those evil forces will continue to remote control your life and destiny.

You must *REPENT* and *CONFESS* & *PROCLAIM* THE LORD JESUS CHRIST

The word says as many as received him, to them gave He power to become the sons of God. Even to them that believe on his name.

To qualify for divine visitation do the following sincerely

1) *Acknowledge* that you are a sinner and that He died for you. **Romans 3:23.**

2) *Repent of your sins.* **Acts 3:19, Luke 13:5, 2 Peter 3:9**

3) *Believe in your heart* that Jesus died for your sin. **Romans 10:10**

4) *Confess Jesus as the Lord over your life.* **Romans 10:10, Acts 2:21**

Now repeat this Prayer after me

Say Lord Jesus, I accept you today, as my Lord and my savior, forgive me of my sins wash me with your blood. Right now, I believe, I am sanctified, I am save, I am free, I am free from the Power of sin to serve the Lord Jesus. Thank you Lord for saving me. Amen. Congratulation: ***YOU ARE NOW A BORN AGAIN CHRISTIAN.***

STEPS TO OVERCOME THE LIFESTYLE OF SIN

1) *FAITH:* No one will overcome a sinful lifestyle without faith. Faith is the catalyst that will push you out of sin. Most prevailing controlling forces will not retreat unless the spirit of faith comes into play. Unless you develop faith, controlling forces has power to prevail. Therefore develop faith that will crush all prevailing remote control forces. I see your faith bring you deliverance over that prevailing lustful situation.

2) *DECISION:* All evil forces know when you make up your mind. In 2006 I found myself in a difficult challenge of my life that it took faith and a decision in 2008 to overcome it. In your life time decisions are vital keys to remain in the flight of success & excellence. Decisions are the pillars to determine the outcome of your life. Most of the things that happened in your lifetime are a function of decision. Decisions are the gateway into your freedom, liberty and a glorious future. When you settle for less, you can only get what is entitled for the less privilege. (See **Luke 16:21**.) Despite all the riches of the father, the prodigal son took a drastic decision that reduced him to eat the pig's food, until he came to himself.... **Luke 15:17**. Although you might not have noticed nor considered

these your lifestyle is wrapped in the decision you make. All of these prevailing forces, that have molded your lifestyle did not happen overnight. At some point in your lifetime, you made a decision and invited certain controlling forces in your life. You are free until you decide to marry. King Solomon was right with God until he decided to go after strange women. (See **1 Kings 11:1-6**.) David brought a sword into his family when he murdered Uriah the Hittite. Take a decision today and evict the old man of sin. (See **Romans 6:1-14**.)

3) ***PRAYER:*** Prayer is crucial especially when you are dealing with dominating forces. Most of the relief and assurance that will come in to your life is on the plat form of prayers. The significance of prayer cannot be over emphasized. Most of us complain about challenges but never create time to pray about it. We tell everybody about it but we do not tell God about it.

HOW TO ACTIVATE THE HOLY SPIRIT IN YOUR LIFE

First of all you must believe that there is a Holy Spirit.

1) ***Acknowledge*** the person of the Holy Spirit.

2) **_Believe_** in the ministration of the Holy Spirit

3) **_Submit_** & **_obey_** the person of the Holy Spirit.

4) **_Welcome_** the sweet presence of the Holy Spirit.

Begin a relationship with the Holy Spirit today and make him your best friend. Never start your day without inviting the person of the Holy Spirit to come into your life.

SUMMARY OF CHAPTER ONE

THE HOLY SPIRIT IS A PERSON OF THE GOD HEAD. God the Father is and Jesus Christ is in heaven, although Jesus Christ is coming soon, he is still in heaven but God the Holy Spirit is here with us. We must all respect and appreciate the daily help of the Holy Spirit in our lives.

The Holy Spirit is a person!

Eccl. 5:6

Suffer not thy mouth to cause thy flesh to sin; neither say thou before the angel, that it was an error: wherefore should God be angry at thy voice, and destroy the work of thine hands?

Therefore watch what you say to him, He demands your attention at all times, yield to him, obey him and give him your time.

Exodus 23:21-22

Beware of him, and obey his voice, provoke him not; for he will not pardon your transgressions: for my name is in him. But if thou shalt indeed obey his voice, and do all that I speak; then I will be an enemy unto thine enemies, and an adversary unto thine adversaries.

He enjoys references and respect. Place him as a senior partner or a big brother. Never come up with excuses why you couldn't respect, reference, acknowledge him. Never use your mouth to wound him by the things you say out aloud.

Remember he is the Holy Spirit, therefore; he demands holiness, quietness, especially when he is talking to you. Always request politely for the Holy Spirit to take the lead and start your day for you. Never engage on any critical decision making without telling your best friend the Holy Spirit.

DECISION KEYS

1) NOTHING CHANGES UNTIL YOU MAKE UP YOUR MIND

2) DECISION IS THE GATEWAY TO DELIVERANCE.

3) UNTIL YOU DECIDE, NO ONE WILL DECIDE FOR YOU.

4) YOUR PROSPERITY IS PROPORTIONAL TO YOUR DECISIONS.

5) THE DECISION YOU MAKE WILL DETERMINE THE FUTURE YOU WILL CREATE

6) DECISION CREATES FUTURE & FULFILLS DESTINIES.

7) DECISION BEAUTIFIES OUR FUTURE.

8) DECISION KEEPS YOU OUT OF TROUBLE

9) DECISION EXEMPTS YOU FROM EVIL

10) DECISION GUARANTEES ETERNITY

11) YOU CAN ONLY GO FAR IN LIFE BY YOUR FAITH DECISIONS.

12) YOU ARE POOR BECAUSE YOU MADE SUCH DECISIONS

13) MAKE A DECISION & CHANGE YOUR LIFE.

14) LIFE CHANGING DECISIONS IS A FUNCTION OF QUALITY INFORMATION

15) SUCCESS IN LIFE IS A FUNCTION OF DECISION.

16) LIFE EXPERIENCES IS FULL OF DECISIONS.

17) DECISIONS CHANGES DESTINIES.

18) NEVER SETTLE FOR INFORMATION ONLY LOOK FOR REVELATION

19) YOU ARE WHERE YOU ARE TODAY BASED ON YOUR LAST DECISION.

20) INFORMATION IS CRUCIAL IN DECISION MAKING

21) DECISION MAKERS RULE THE WORLD.

22) YOU CAN RULE YOUR WORLD BY QUALITY DECISIONS

23) AS LONG AS YOU DECIDE RIGHTLY SATAN CANNOT HARASS YOU.

CHAPTER 2

THE WORKS & OPERATION OF THE HOLY SPIRIT

Acts 2:4

And they were all filled with the Holy Ghost and began to speak with other tongues, as the Spirit gave them utterance.

Although the Holy Spirit is the Spirit of life, he is also the Spirit of conviction and fellowship. In these end times there is much work that the Holy Spirit is doing today that we do not recognize. In these dreadful days of gross darkness, terrorist and destruction of lives and properties worldwide, we cannot forsake the operations & works of the Holy Spirit.

Without argument the Holy Spirit is the anointing of God that grants boldness and authority. Every anointed man/woman of God is a vessel with the abundance of the Holy Spirit. The Holy Spirit empowers you for enthronement. Nevertheless, this is the same Spirit of the Lord that PREVAILED for Samson against the Philistines

Acts 1:8

But ye shall receive power, after that the Holy Ghost is come upon you, and ye shall be witnesses unto me both in Jerusalem, and in all Judea, and in Samaria, and unto the uttermost part of the earth.

A greater portion of the assignment of the Holy Spirit is to reveal, counter attack and restore any stolen item by the devil. As you can remember, the devil came to kill, to steal and to destroy.

THE FUNCTIONS & POSITIONS OF THE HOLY SPIRIT

1) ***OVERSEER:*** The Holy Spirit is the overseer of the Church of Jesus Christ. He over sees all activities of the church, protects the Church of Jesus Christ against the forces of hell. *The Bible says take heed therefore unto yourselves, and to all the flock, over the Holy Ghost hath made you overseers, to feed the church of God, which he hath purchased with his own blood.*

2) ***FELLOWSHIP:*** **1 John 1:7** *But if we walk in the light, as he is in the light, we have fellowship one with another, and the blood of Jesus Christ his Son cleanseth us from all sin.* We cannot have genuine fellowship with the father without the help of the Holy Spirit. The Bible says create in me a clean heart, O God; and renew a right spirit within me. Cast me not away from thy presence; and take not thy holy spirit from me. Restore unto me the joy of thy salvation; and uphold me with thy free spirit. Furthermore the Bible says *Likewise the Spirit also helpeth our infirmities: for we know not what we should pray for as we ought: but the Spirit itself maketh intercession for us with groanings which cannot be uttered.*

3) ***REPROOFS***: Have you been walking in ignorance and in error? Humble your selves and call on the Holy Spirit. The only person who can correct you quickly is the Holy Spirit. **Psalms 51:12** *Restore unto me the joy of thy salvation; and uphold me with thy free spirit. The Bible says turn you at my reproof: behold, I will pour out my spirit unto you, I will make known my words unto you.*

4) ***INSTRUCTOR:*** The Almighty was referring to the Holy Spirit when the Bible says *I will instruct thee and*

teach thee in the way which thou shalt go: I will guide thee with mine eye. Contrary to what we believe and think, all heavenly instructions from the father through the mediator is delivered by the Holy Spirit. The Holy Spirit instructs us in time of trouble, confusion and error. **Nehemiah 9:20** *Thou gavest also thy good spirit to instruct them, and withheldest not thy manna from their mouth, and gavest them water for their thirst.*

5) *DIRECTOR:* With all humility before God, all intend of the hearts, what you plan to do, what you are thinking and engaging your mind on, is all by the help of the Holy Spirit. **Phil 2:13** *For it is God which worketh in you both to will and to do of his good pleasure. For in him we live, and move, and have our being; as certain also of your own poets have said, For we are also his offspring.*

6) *CONVICTS:* No man/woman can go far in life without the help of the Holy Spirit. Genuine conviction can only come by the Holy Spirit. **John 16:7-11** *Nevertheless I tell you the truth; It is expedient for you that I go away: for if I go not away, the Comforter will not come unto you; but if I depart, I will send him unto you. And when he is come, he will reprove the world of sin, and of righteousness, and of judgment: Of sin, because they believe not on me;*

Of righteousness, because I go to my Father, and ye see me no more; Of judgment, because the prince of this world is judged.

7) **_PRICKS THE HEART:_** THE ONLY PERSON WHO CAN GENUINELY CAUSE US TO REPENT IS THE HOLY SPIRIT. Genuine repentance and conviction is possible by the help of the Holy Spirit. Now when they heard this, they were pricked in their heart, and said unto Peter and to the rest of the apostles, Men and brethren, what shall we do? Then Peter said unto them, Repent, and be baptized every one of you in the name of Jesus Christ for the remission of sins, and ye shall receive the gift of the Holy Ghost.

8) **_JUDGMENT:_** Every time the policeman of the heart is judging your action is by the conviction of the Holy Spirit. **John 16:8-11** *And when he is come, he will reprove the world of sin, and of righteousness, and of judgment: Of sin, because they believe not on me; Of righteousness, because I go to my Father, and ye see me no more; Of judgment, because the prince of this world is judged. And I will put my spirit within you, and cause you to walk in my statutes, and ye shall keep my judgments, and do them.*

9) *GUIDANCE:* We are helpless without the help of the Holy Spirit. Genuine guidance can only come by the help of the Holy Spirit. **Psalms 32:8** *...I will guide thee with mine eye. Genuine guidance comes from the Lord Almighty. Thus saith the Lord, thy Redeemer, the Holy One of Israel; I am the Lord thy God which teacheth thee to profit, which leadeth thee by the way that thou shouldest go.* When God is leading us, it does not come with struggles nor hardship. ***And they thirsted not when he led them through the deserts: he caused the waters to flow out of the rock for them: he clave the rock also, and the waters gushed out.***

THE HOLY SPIRIT IS THE UNQUENCHABLE FIRE

Matthew 3:11-12

I indeed baptize you with water unto repentance. but he that cometh after me is mightier than I, whose shoes I am not worthy to bear: he shall baptize you with the Holy Ghost, and with fire:

Whose fan is in his hand, and he will thoroughly purge his floor, and gather his wheat into the garner; but he will burn up the chaff with unquenchable fire.

The Holy Spirit is the anointing of God....You may ask why?

...Because the Spirit of the Lord rests upon the anointing.

1 John 2:20

But ye have an unction from the Holy One, and ye know all things. (Also See 1 Sam. 16:13-14.)

THE HOLY SPIRIT IS THE REFINERS FIRE

Malachi 3:1-3

Behold, I will send my messenger, and he shall prepare the way before me: and the Lord, whom ye seek, shall suddenly come to his temple, even the messenger of the covenant, whom ye delight in: behold, he shall come, saith the Lord of hosts.

*But who may abide the day of his coming? and who shall stand when he appeareth? **for he is like a refiner's fire, and like fullers' soap:***

And he shall sit as a refiner and purifier of silver: and he shall purify the sons of Levi, and purge them as gold and silver, that they may offer unto the Lord an offering in righteousness.

THE HOLY SPIRIT IS THE SPIRIT OF LIFE

Romans 8:2

For the law of the Spirit of life in Christ Jesus hath made me free from the law of sin and death.

HIGHLIGHTS TO ACTIVATE THE WORKS OF THE HOLY SPIRIT

1) **PURIFICATION**: There is no substitute to holy living. As long as you are living in purification and sanctification, you are a candidate for the works and operation of the Holy Spirit. **John 9:31** says *God heareth not sinners....* In my own interpretation the Holy Spirit ignores all sinners. Sanctification is the plat form for the works of the Holy Spirit. As long as there is sin in your life, the Holy Spirit will not manifest through you and in you.

2) **QUICKENING POWER**: The reason for all the delays in your life is because the Holy Spirit have not

manifested over your circumstance. **1 Cor. 12:7** But the manifestation of the Spirit is given to every man to profit withal. **Romans 8:11** *But if the Spirit of him that raised up Jesus from the dead dwell in you, he that raised up Christ from the dead shall also quicken your mortal bodies by his Spirit that dwelleth in you.*

3) ***EMPOWERMENT:*** Almost all the heroes of faith in the Bible were empowered by the Holy Ghost: The Bible says how God anointed Jesus of Nazareth with HOLY GHOST and with POWER: who went about doing good, and healing all that were oppressed of the devil, for God was with him. The reason the Apostles prevailed and it was noised abroad (**Acts 2:6**) was simply because… **Acts 2:4** *…And there appeared unto them cloven tongues like as of fire, and it sat upon each of them. And they were all filled with the Holy Ghost, and began to speak with other tongues, as the Spirit gave them utterance.*

CONDITION TO RECEIVE THE HOLY SPIRIT

1) ***REPENTANCE:*** Repent, and be baptized every one of you in the name of Jesus Christ for the remission of sins, and ye shall receive the gift of the Holy Ghost.

2) **BE BAPTIZED:** ...be baptized every one of you in the name of Jesus Christ for the remission of sins, and ye shall receive the gift of the Holy Ghost

3) **CONFESS OF YOUR SIN:** If we confess our sins, he is faithful and just to forgive us our sins, and to cleanse us from all unrighteousness.

4) **ACKNOWLEDGMENT:** Acknowledge that you are a sinner and that Jesus Christ died for your sins. **Romans 3:23.**

5) **BORN AGAIN:** John 3:3-8 *Jesus answered and said unto him, Verily, verily, I say unto thee, Except a man be born again, he cannot see the kingdom of God. Nicodemus saith unto him, How can a man be born when he is old? can he enter the second time into his mother's womb, and be born? Jesus answered, Verily, verily, I say unto thee, Except a man be born of water and of the Spirit, he cannot enter into the kingdom of God. That which is born of the flesh is flesh; and that which is born of the Spirit is spirit. Marvel not that I said unto thee, Ye must be born again. The wind bloweth where it listeth, and thou hearest the sound thereof, but canst not tell whence it cometh, and whither it goeth: so is every one that is born of the Spirit.*

CHAPTER 3

THE GUIDANCE & ACQUAINTANCE OF THE HOLY SPIRIT

Nehemiah 9:20

Thou gavest also thy good spirit to instruct them, and withheldest not thy manna from their mouth, and gavest them water for their thirst.

Although the Holy Spirit leads us all, the Holy Spirit of God does not lead sinners in my own scriptural understanding. For as many as are led by the Spirit of God, they are the sons of God. The Spirit itself beareth witness with our spirit, that we are the children of God: There is no guarantee for the covering and guidance of the Holy Spirit, as long as you are walking in sin.

The companionship of the Holy Spirit only comes with great requirements. The Holy Spirit is a very strong personality who demands righteousness, holiness, integrity honesty and truth. The principal assignment of the Holy Spirit is to guide us against satanic wiles and scheme. When the almighty God made this profound statement, He was referring to the Holy Spirit.

Psalms 32:8

I will guide thee with mine eye.

CONDITIONS FOR THE ACQUAINTANCE OF THE HOLY SPIRIT

1) *WALKING IN THE SPIRIT:* As long as you operate and walk in the Spirit, you will forever carry divine presence of the Holy Spirit. *If we live in the Spirit, let us also walk in the Spirit.* There is a great presence when you walk and operate in the Spirit. This I say then, Walk in the Spirit, and ye shall not fulfill the lust of the flesh. For the flesh lusteth against the Spirit, and the Spirit against the flesh: and these are contrary the one to the other: so that ye cannot do the things that ye would. But if ye be led of the Spirit, ye are not under the law. We must walk in the Spirit in order to receive the things which are of the Spirit. But the natural man receiveth not the things of the Spirit of God: for they are foolishness unto him: neither can he know them, because they are spiritually discerned.

2) ***FAITH:*** It takes faith to maintain the acquaintance and guidance of the Holy Spirit. The Holy Spirit is the Spirit of faith that encourages you in time of trouble. **2 Cor. 4:13** We having the same spirit of faith, according as it is written, I believed, and therefore have I spoken; we also believe, and therefore speak.

3) ***WALK IN AGREEMENT:*** We must walk in agreement with Holy Spirit in order to provoke his guidance and acquaintance. The Bible says... *Again I say unto you, That if two of you shall agree on earth as touching anything that they shall ask, it shall be done for them of my Father which is in heaven. Can two walk together, except they both agreed?* **Amos 3:3**

4) ***WALK IN LOVE:*** Most of us want the Holy Spirit as our friend but yet we are filled with bitterness, grudge and anger. The Holy Spirit by definition is a HOLY..... **1 John 4:16** *And we have known and believed the love that God hath to us. God is love; and he that dwelleth in love dwelleth in God, and God in him.*

5) ***WALK IN TRUTH:*** The Holy Spirit is the Spirit of truth and therefore despise all liars. **John 16:13** *Howbeit when he, the Spirit of truth, is come, he will guide you into*

all truth: for he shall not speak of himself; but whatsoever he shall hear, that shall he speak: and he will shew you things to come. The Holy Spirit will flee from your presence as long as you carry a lying tongue.

SUMMARY OF CHAPTER 3

THE GUIDANCE & ACQUAINTANCE OF THE HOLY SPIRIT

The one million dollar question here is, do you truly desire the person of the Holy Spirit? If you consciously answered yes to the above question you must pray and demand for His manifestation into your life. The Holy Spirit is pleased with people that walk in truth, endowed with integrity, righteousness, holiness, fear of the Lord, honest, humble meek, love God, soul winners, and believes in the person and ministry of the Holy Spirit.

As long as you are proud and arrogant in your speech, the Holy Spirit will forever be far from your life. The Holy Spirit is looking for the meek.

Psalms 25:9

The meek will he guide in judgment: and the meek will he teach his way.

The guidance and acquaintance of the Holy Spirit makes you a witness. Remember he is the Spirit of life and the Spirit of witness. For the law of the Spirit of life in Christ Jesus hath made me free from the law of sin and death.

CHAPTER 4

ENJOYING THE LEADERSHIP OF THE HOLY SPIRIT

ACTS 16:6-7

Now when they had gone throughout Phrygia and the region of Galatia, and were forbidden of the Holy Ghost to preach the word in Asia, After they were come to Mysia, they assayed to go into Bithynia: but the Spirit suffered them not.

Although there are only two Kingdom, we belong to one Kingdom per time. When we became born again Christians, **Colossians 1:13** says *Who hath delivered us from the power of darkness, and hath translated us into the kingdom of his dear Son.* Every time you end up in shame, fear destruction and hardship you are being led by the evil spirit. The leadership of the Holy Spirit is a confirming spirit. The Holy Spirit cannot be in charge of your life without a confirmation. *The Bible says the Spirit itself beareth witness with our spirit, that we are the children of God.*

Briefly, let's examine the benefits of the leadership of the Holy Spirit:

1) *PEACE:* Every time you are led by the Holy Spirit there is inner peace and serenity. The peace we are talking here grants comfort, assurance and rest. **2 Thess. 3:16** Now the Lord of peace himself give you peace always by all means. The Lord be with you all. These peace of mind in my opinion comes only from the Holy Spirit. **Phil 4:7** *And the peace of God, which passeth all understanding, shall keep your hearts and minds through Christ Jesus.* The peace of mind we are talking here is the peace that emerges in the midst of trial and tribulation. This is the peace of mind that dominates all prevailing obstacles and challenges against your rising. I see that PEACE come upon you in Jesus Name. **John 20:21-22** *Then said Jesus to them again, Peace be unto you: as my Father hath sent me, even so send I you. And when he had said this, he breathed on them, and saith unto them, Receive ye the Holy Ghost:*

2) *ENDURANCE:* The leadership of the Holy Spirit comes with endurance. Every time you are anxious and impatient that is not the Holy Spirit. The book of **Hebrews** chapter **12:2** confirms to us that the Holy Spirit is an enduring Spirit. **Hebrews 12:2** *Looking unto Jesus*

the author and finisher of our faith; who for the joy that was set before him endured the cross, despising the shame, and is set down at the right hand of the throne of God. As long as you are being led by the Holy Spirit, the ability to endure difficulty, tribulation, fear and torment is provoked without your consciousness. **Mark 13:13** *And ye shall be hated of all men for my name's sake: but he that shall endure unto the end, the same shall be saved.*

3) ***JOY:*** Most of us believers does not realize that when the Holy Spirit is in control, He takes away all the pains, the fear, the torture and the agony. Every time we are anxious for what will happen, or how it will happen, it is not the Holy Spirit. There is a unique JOY that dominates our SPIRIT when the Holy Spirit is in control. The leadership of the Holy Spirit comes with a JOY, which Apostle Peter called Joy unspeakable full of glory. **1 Peter 1:8** *Whom having not seen, ye love; in whom, though now ye see him not, yet believing, ye rejoice with joy unspeakable and full of glory*: Embrace the leadership of the Holy Spirit and enjoy this lasting joy in your life. **Psalms 16:11** *Thou wilt shew me the path of life: in thy presence is fullness of joy; at thy right hand there are pleasures for evermore.*

4) **_FAITH:_** The primary test to double check on who is leading you is the presence of faith and no fear in your life. Peter began to walk on water once faith rose up in him, but when he got into the natural he began to sink. **Matthew 14:27-30** *But straightway Jesus spake unto them, saying, Be of good cheer; it is I; be not afraid. And Peter answered him and said, Lord, if it be thou, bid me come unto thee on the water. And he said, Come. And when Peter was come down out of the ship, he walked on the water, to go to Jesus. But when he saw the wind boisterous, he was afraid; and beginning to sink, he cried, saying, Lord, save me.* The faith here is the absence of fear. The leadership of the Holy Spirit provides the Faith that destroys mountain, diminish prevailing obstacles and conquer giants. Without this faith we cannot please God. **Hebrews 11:6** *But without faith it is impossible to please him: for he that cometh to God must believe that he is, and that he is a rewarder of them that diligently seek him.*

5) **_REVELATION:_** The leadership of the Holy Spirit comes with revelation of Gods secret. **Rev. 1:10** *I was in the Spirit on the Lord's day, and heard behind me a great voice, as of a trumpet.* All prophets of God prophesied only when

moved by the Holy Spirit. **2 Peter 1:21** *For the prophecy came not in old time by the will of man: but holy men of God spake as they were moved by the Holy Ghost.* However, the natural man cannot receive revelation because they are spiritually discerned. **1 Cor. 2:13-14** *Which things also we speak, not in the words which man's wisdom teacheth, but which the Holy Ghost teacheth; comparing spiritual things with spiritual. But the natural man receiveth not the things of the Spirit of God: for they are foolishness unto him: neither can he know them, because they are spiritually discerned.* Apostle Paul because he was a man filled with the Holy Ghost, there was abundance of revelation for him to un-fold. **2 Cor. 12:7** *And lest I should be exalted above measure through the abundance of the revelations…* May you surrender your life today and embrace the leadership of the Holy Spirit. May I say this allow God to lead you from hence forth

6) *LOVE:* The leadership of the Holy Spirit comes with a convicting and compelling LOVE. The Bible says for *God so LOVED, he gave…* (See **John 3:16**.) Every time you love , it is confirmed by your ability to giving. The Love here is that love that makes faith to work. **Gal. 5:6** *…but faith which worketh by love.*

This is the LOVE that takes wipes away shame and plants in confidence and HOPE inside of you. **Romans 5:5** *And hope maketh not ashamed; because the love of God is shed abroad in our hearts by the Holy Ghost which is given unto us.*

WHO DOES THE HOLY SPIRIT LEAD?

1 Cor. 12:7

But the manifestation of the Spirit is given to every man to profit withal

The Holy Spirit is a liberal Spirit, therefore He is open to all. **Proverbs 11:25** *The liberal soul shall be made fat: and he that watereth shall be watered also himself.* The Holy Spirit will lead all including:

1) THE MEEK

2) THE HUMBLE

3) THOSE THAT FEAR GOD

4) THOSE WHO WALK IN LOVE & AGREEMENT

5) THE SPIRITUAL

6) THE RIGHTEOUS

7) THE FAITHFUL

2 Cor. 3:17-17

Now the Lord is that Spirit: and where the Spirit of the Lord is, there is liberty. This liberty here is your ability to embrace holiness as a lifestyle. **Gal. 5:25** *If we live in the Spirit, let us also walk in the Spirit.*

To live in the Spirit and to walk in the Spirit means to live a righteous lifestyle, forsake sin and present your body a living sacrifice for the Lord Jesus Christ.

Gal. 5:16

This I say then, Walk in the Spirit, and ye shall not fulfill the lust of the flesh.

The Holy Spirit will not lead any sinner until they repent from their heart. *Turn you at my reproof: behold, I will pour out my spirit unto you, I will make known my words unto you.* As long as you recognize Jesus Christ as Lord and you despise not the Holy Spirit, he will lead you.

HINDRANCE TO RECEIVING THE HOLY SPIRIT

1) **BITTERNESS:** As long as you are bitter within, I mean you harbor bitterness in your heart, you hinder the Holy Spirit from manifesting in your life. Holy Spirit demands a peaceful atmosphere, therefore as long as you are bitter, you walk around with hatred and jealously and envy inside of your heart, The Holy Spirit is very far away from you. **Hebrews 12:15** *Looking diligently lest any man fail of the grace of God; lest any root of bitterness springing up trouble you, and thereby many be defiled;*

2) **INIQUITY:** As long as you constantly live in sin, the Holy Spirit will stay far away from you. **Job 22:21-24** *Acquaint now thyself with him, and be at peace: thereby good shall come unto thee. Receive, I pray thee, the law from his mouth, and lay up his words in thine heart. If thou return to the Almighty, thou shalt be built up, thou shalt put away iniquity far from thy tabernacles. Then shalt thou lay up gold as dust, and the gold of Ophir as the stones of the brooks.* Iniquity is constant repetition of sin. God hears all your supplication but iniquity creates a distance between you and the Holy Spirit. **Isaiah 59:1-2**

Behold, the Lord's hand is not shortened, that it cannot save; neither his ear heavy that it cannot hear: But your iniquities have separated between you and your God, and your sins have hid his face from you, that he will not hear.

3) **UN-FORGIVENESS:** Un-forgiveness is an opening of the enemy to drive away the Holy Spirit. We easily ask for forgiveness from others, while we all hold others in contempt against the wrong they did to us. The lifestyle of un-forgiveness is a strong hold that hinders the Holy Spirit. **Matthew 6:14-15** *For if ye forgive men their trespasses, your heavenly Father will also forgive you: But if ye forgive not men their trespasses, neither will your Father forgive your trespasses.* **Jeremiah 31:34** *... for I will forgive their iniquity, and I will remember their sin no more.*

4) **REGRET:** One great man once said and I quote" when you are depressed, you are living in the past, when you are anxious you are living in the future, but when you are at PEACE you are living in the present." **Isaiah 43:18-19** *Remember ye not the former things, neither consider the things of old. Behold, I will do a new thing; now it shall spring forth; shall ye*

not know it? I will even make a way in the wilderness, and rivers in the desert. Living in regret drives away the presence of the Holy Spirit. In this race of life, you cannot accomplish nor achieve anything tangible in life as long as you keep memorizing your short coming, past failures and lost moments, gods and money. The Holy Spirit is not excited when you memorize misery and failure seasons of your life.

ACCESS TO RECEIVE THE PERSON OF THE HOLY SPIRIT

1) ***BE BORN AGAIN:*** In these evil days, full of terror, it is easy to tell when un-believer is going through trial and tribulation. As long as you are not a born again Christian all you will get is "sorriooo" and a mere word of comfort "it is well with you "off-course you know it shall not be well with you. We established earlier that the Holy Spirit does not lead sinners. The Spirit of the Lord comes a fresh and becomes a reality once you confess Jesus Christ as your Lord and savior. **John 3:3-8** *Jesus answered and said unto him, Verily, verily, I say unto thee, Except a man be born again, he cannot see the kingdom of God. Nicodemus saith unto him, How*

can a man be born when he is old? can he enter the second time into his mother's womb, and be born? Jesus answered, Verily, verily, I say unto thee, Except a man be born of water and of the Spirit, he cannot enter into the kingdom of God. That which is born of the flesh is flesh; and that which is born of the Spirit is spirit. Marvel not that I said unto thee, Ye must be born again. The wind bloweth where it listeth, and thou hearest the sound thereof, but canst not tell whence it cometh, and whither it goeth: so is every one that is born of the Spirit. Until you confess, acknowledge the Lord Jesus as your savior you will forever be subdued with trials and tribulation. Eternity is real therefore if you are not a born again Christian, do so quickly before concluding this Holy Spirit revealed manual.

2) **THE FEAR OF GOD:** You must develop the consciousness of the fear of God in your heart if you desire to overcome trials and tribulation. As long as you fear God, the help of the Holy Spirit is on the way. The Lord made it clear it shall be well with the righteous but it shall not be well with the wicked. **Eccl. 8:12-13** *Though a sinner do evil an hundred times, and his days be prolonged, yet surely I know that it shall be well with*

them that fear God, which fear before him: But it shall not be well with the wicked, neither shall he prolong his days, which are as a shadow; because he feareth not before God. The Holy Spirit will choose you, to teach you all things once you embrace the fear of God in your life. **Psalms 25:12** *What man is he that feareth the Lord? him shall he teach in the way that he shall choose.*

3) ***RIGHTEOUS LIFESTYLE:*** As long as you practice a righteous lifestyle, you will forever enjoy the presence of the Holy Spirit. **1 John 3:7** Little children, let no man deceive you: he that doeth righteousness is righteous, even as he is righteous. **Isaiah 32:17** *And the work of righteousness shall be peace; and the effect of righteousness quietness and assurance forever.* Righteousness is the access key to provoke the presence of the Holy Spirit.

4) ***INTEGRITY:*** In my own simplified words, the spirit of integrity is the truth. The Holy Spirit is the spirit of truth therefore the Holy Spirit enjoys everyone who speak and carries the mantle of the truth in their life. In this race of life integrity is the access key to provoke the person of the Holy Spirit. **Proverbs 11:3** *The integrity of the upright shall guide them....*

5) ***AGREEMENT:*** The Bible says Can two walk together unless they be agreed. **Amos 3:3** *Can two walk together, except they be agreed?* Agreement is the access gateway for the person of the Holy Spirit. **Matthew 18:16** vs **19-20** *But if he will not hear thee, then take with thee one or two more, that in the mouth of two or three witnesses every word may be established. Verily I say unto you, Whatsoever ye shall bind on earth shall be bound in heaven: and whatsoever ye shall loose on earth shall be loosed in heaven. Again I say unto you, That if two of you shall agree on earth as touching any thing that they shall ask, it shall be done for them of my Father which is in heaven. For where two or three are gathered together in my name, there am I in the midst of them.*

6) ***THE RIGHT WORDS:*** Every time you speak the right word the Holy Spirit comes into your life. **Job 6:25** declares *How forcible are right words!* Jesus said there is no idle word in the kingdom. Every time you speak, your words are judged by the angels of the living God. **Eccl. 5:6** *Suffer not thy mouth to cause thy flesh to sin; neither say thou before the angel, that it was an error: wherefore should God be angry at thy voice, and destroy the work of thine hands?* The right words will bring you

out of captivity, the right word will provoke the Holy Spirit to come for your rescue.

7) ***SOUL WINNING:*** Until you join force with Jesus to enforce the great commission to win souls for His kingdom, the Holy Spirit will forever be far from you. **Matthew 28:18-20** *And Jesus came and spake unto them, saying, All power is given unto me in heaven and in earth. Go ye therefore, and teach all nations, baptizing them in the name of the Father, and of the Son, and of the Holy Ghost: Teaching them to observe all things whatsoever I have commanded you: and, lo, I am with you always, even unto the end of the world. Amen.*

8) ***OBEDIENCE:*** As long as you are walking in disobedience you will never experience the manifestation of the Holy Spirit. Remember he is the seal of redemption. **Ephesians 1:13** *In whom ye also trusted, after that ye heard the word of truth, the gospel of your salvation: in whom also after that ye believed, ye were sealed with that holy Spirit of promise.* **Hebrews 13:17** *Obey them that have the rule over you, and submit yourselves: for they watch for your souls, as they that must give account, that they may do it with joy, and not with grief: for that is unprofitable for you.*

9) ***PRAY IN THE SPIRIT:*** When you pray in the SPIRIT you are not speaking to men but unto GOD. **1 Cor. 14:2** *For he that speaketh in an unknown tongue speaketh not unto men, but unto God: for no man understandeth him; howbeit in the spirit he speaketh mysteries.*

WAYS IN WHICH THE HOLY SPIRIT LEADS & DIRECTS US:

1) ***AUDIBLE VOICE:*** The Holy Spirit speaks to us. The Bible says in **Acts 10:19** *while peter thought on the vision the Holy Spirit said unto him, Behold three men seek thee.* **Acts 13:2** *As they ministered to the Lord, and fasted, the Holy Ghost said, Separate me Barnabas and Saul for the work whereunto I have called them.* If you are not in the Spirit you can get into the spirit by singing a heavenly son unto the Holy Spirit.

This I called melody.

MELODY: Every time you sing unto the Lord you are bound to hear His voice in a song or melody. Through singing sweet songs late at night or early in the morning. **Isaiah 30:29** *And the Lord shall cause his glorious voice to be heard, and shall shew the lighting down of his arm,* *with the indignation of his anger, and with the flame of a devouring fire, with scattering, and tempest, and hailstones. For through the voice of the Lord shall the Assyrian be beaten down, which smote with a rod.* **Isaiah 51:3** For the Lord shall comfort Zion: he will comfort all her waste places; and he will make her wilderness like Eden, and her desert like the garden of the Lord; joy and gladness shall be found therein, thanksgiving, and the voice of melody. You provoke the Holy Spirit into action once you lift up spiritual songs to minister to the Spirit. **Acts 10:44** ***While Peter yet spake these words, the Holy Ghost fell on all them which heard the word.***

2) ***THROUGH THY WORD:*** Every life question and answer is in the Bible. Abbreviated B.I.B.L.E.

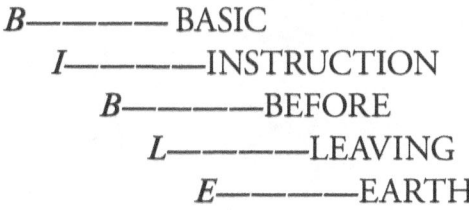

```
B——————— BASIC
    I———————INSTRUCTION
    B———————BEFORE
        L———————LEAVING
            E———————EARTH
```

The word of God is the only life applicable manual relevant in all ages for all mean and for all times. The Bible is the most referenced book for businesses, government

establishment, marriage institution and all aspect of life.
Psalms 119:10 *Thy word is a lamp unto my feet, and a light unto my path.*

SUMMARY OF CHAPTER 4

ENJOYING THE LEADERSHIP OF THE HOLY SPIRIT

The Holy Spirit is your leader, therefore as a follower you are bound to obey His leadership. **Hebrews 13:17** *Obey them that have the rule over you, and submit yourselves: for they watch for your souls, as they that must give account, that they may do it with joy, and not with grief: for that is unprofitable for you.*

If you truly desire to enjoy the leadership of the Holy Spirit then you must do the following:

1) ***PRAY IN THE SPIRIT:*** There is a refreshing that overcomes over your spirit man once you pray in the SPIRIT. **Acts 2:2-4** *And suddenly there came a sound from heaven as of a rushing mighty wind, and it filled all the house where they were sitting. And there appeared unto them cloven tongues like as of fire, and it sat upon each of them. And they were all filled with the Holy Ghost, and began to speak with other tongues, as the Spirit gave them utterance.* When you pray in the SPIRIT you are not speaking to men but unto GOD. **1 Cor. 14:2** *For he that speaketh in an unknown*

tongue speaketh not unto men, but unto God: for no man understandeth him; howbeit in the spirit he speaketh mysteries.

CHAPTER 5

OVERCOMING TRIALS BY THE HELP OF THE HOLY SPIRIT

John 16:33

These things I have spoken unto you, that in me ye might have peace. In the world ye shall have tribulation: but be of good cheer; I have overcome the world.

Although we live and operate in a physical kingdom where trial and temptation is bound to come to pass in our life time. God gave us the precious Holy Spirit to strengthen and minister to us in time of trouble. As long as you live temptation and trial will come. But thank God for victory. **1 Cor. 10:13** *There hath no temptation taken you but such as is common to man: but God is faithful, who will not suffer you to be tempted above that ye are able; but will with the temptation also make a way to escape, that ye may be able to bear it.*

My mentor once said that life is in phases while men are in seizes. In my own view, every level in life, comes with a challenge. Just like my mentor used to say, there is no mountain anywhere in the world, your present mountain is your ignorance. Information is the relevant access code to breakthrough in that level. The access key here is relevant information that is life transforming.

The accomplished milestone in your life is the result of the available information to your reach. Ask the Holy Spirit to make you access relevant information to overcome any present challenge, trial and tribulation. Engage the Holy Spirit as your very present help in all times and not only in times of trouble. At every level of your life there is always a challenge, an obstacle to conquer. It has been proven, as long as you have the companionship of the Holy Spirit you will overcome that prevailing challenge.

Psalms 121:1-2

I will lift up mine eyes unto the hills, from whence cometh my help. My help cometh from the Lord, which made heaven and earth.

As long as you take the Holy Spirit serious in your life, God will also take you serious. Jesus made it clear to us all,

John 16:33 *These things I have spoken unto you, that in me ye might have peace. In the world ye shall have tribulation: but be of good cheer; I have overcome the world.* That you are now a born again, fire baptize, speaks in tongue and in the Holy Ghost does not exempt you from experiencing life challenges.

As a believer you have the privilege to acquaint your life with the help of the Holy Spirit, (See **John 14:18, 26**) you have the accreditation as a spiritual law enforcement office to evict demons far away from your life. You have the last weapon the blood of Jesus to overcome Satan and his cohorts, more also we have the power of attorney in the Name of Jesus. **John 14:13-14** *And whatsoever ye shall ask in my name, that will I do, that the Father may be glorified in the Son. If ye shall ask any thing in my name, I will do it.*

The summary of the trial and tribulations of life is your ability to understand life from a spiritual perspective. Life will not favor you until you are ready to put up a fight. **1 Timothy 6:12** *Fight the good fight of faith, lay hold on eternal life, whereunto thou art also called, and hast professed a good profession before many witnesses.*

"What you do not want, you don't watch".
"What you do not resist has power to remain".
"What you do not confront, you cannot conquer."

These few quote is the solution to every challenge you will ever encounter in life. Most of our short coming is inability to confront challenging situations.

Briefly let's examine the prerequisite to overcome trial and tribulation in life.

1) **BE BORN AGAIN:** In these evil days, full of terror, it is easy to tell when un-believer is going through trial and tribulation. As long as you are not a born again Christian all you will get is "sorriooo" and a mere word of comfort "it is well with you "off-course you know it shall not be well with you. We established earlier that the Holy Spirit does not lead sinners. The Spirit of the Lord comes a fresh and becomes a reality once you confess Jesus Christ as your Lord and savior. **John 3:3-8** *Jesus answered and said unto him, Verily, verily, I say unto thee, Except a man be born again, he cannot see the kingdom of God. Nicodemus saith unto him, How can a man be born when he is old? can he enter the second time into his mother's womb, and be born? Jesus answered, Verily, verily, I say unto thee, Except a man be born of water and of the Spirit, he cannot enter into the kingdom of God. That which is born of the flesh is flesh; and that which is born of the Spirit is spirit. Marvel not that I said unto thee, Ye must be born again. The wind bloweth*

where it listeth, and thou hearest the sound thereof, but canst not tell whence it cometh, and whither it goeth: so is every one that is born of the Spirit. Until you confess, acknowledge the Lord Jesus as your savior you will forever be subdued with trials and tribulation. Eternity is real therefore if you are not a born again Christian, do so quickly before concluding this Holy Spirit revealed manual.

2) ***THE FEAR OF GOD:*** You must develop the consciousness of the fear of God in your heart if you desire to overcome trials and tribulation. As long as you fear God, the help of the Holy Spirit is on the way. The Lord made it clear it shall be well with the righteous but it shall not be well with the wicked. **Eccl. 8:12-13** *Though a sinner do evil an hundred times, and his days be prolonged, yet surely I know that it shall be well with them that fear God, which fear before him: But it shall not be well with the wicked, neither shall he prolong his days, which are as a shadow; because he feareth not before God.* The Holy Spirit will choose you, to teach you all things once you embrace the fear of God in your life. **Psalms 25:12** *What man is he that feareth the Lord? him shall he teach in the way that he shall choose.*

3) **_BOLDNESS:_** Always be bold to go before God and ask him of help and demand the presence of the Holy Spirit. **Hebrews 4:16** Let us therefore come boldly unto the throne of grace that we may obtain mercy, and find grace to help in time of need. Every believer has the accreditation by the blood of Jesus to exercise boldness in all area of our lives. Until you put up boldness, your prevailing obstacle has power to remain. I summon you to gather boldness and allow the Holy Spirit to destroy that hindering obstacle in your life in the name of Jesus. **Acts 14:31** *And when they had prayed, the place was shaken where they were assembled together; and they were all filled with the Holy Ghost, and they spake the word of God with boldness.*

4) **_AUTHORITY:_** Often times we forget who is in charge. Jesus fulfilled his precious promise to send the Holy Spirit to help us here on earth. **John 16:7** Nevertheless I tell you the truth; It is expedient for you that I go away: for if I go not away, the Comforter will not come unto you; but if I depart, I will send him unto you. In my own opinion the Holy Spirit delivers the necessary authority to confront prevailing and challenging obstacles. Therefore gather authority and destroy that prevailing circumstance in your life. **Luke 9:1** *Then he called his twelve disciples*

together, and gave them power and authority over all devils, and to cure diseases.

5) **HAVE FAITH IN GOD:** It takes faith to overcome trials and tribulation in life: **Hebrews 11:6** *But without faith it is impossible to please him: for he that cometh to God must believe that he is, and that he is a rewarder of them that diligently seek him.* The reason God will grant you victory is because you pleased Him. Remember **Proverbs 16:7** *When a man's ways please the Lord, he maketh even his enemies to be at peace with him.*

6) **BE IN AGREEMENT WITH THE HOLY SPIRIT:** The Holy Spirit will leave you alone to solve your problem when you walk in dies-agreement. As long as you are in disagreement you are on your own. Come into agreement today with the Holy Spirit and let him take over all your troubles and hardship. **Amos 3:3** *Can two walk together, except they be agreed?*

7) **DEVELOP A WINNING MENTALITY:** To develop a winning mentality means to go all out for victory by all righteous means. One great man once said that you cannot climb the ladder of success dressed in the custom of failure. Most winners do not quite, remember quitters do

not win. To overcome your present trials and tribulation means you must confront all life challenging issues as they come into your life. The Bible says in **John 16:33** ***These things I have spoken unto you, that in me ye might have peace. In the world ye shall have tribulation: but be of good cheer; I have overcome the world.***

8) ***ENDURANCE:*** No matter the trial and level of tribulation, never give up in your quest to overcome your present trials. As long as you can endure to the end, the sky is your limit. **Matthew 10:22** *And ye shall be hated of all men for my name's sake: but he that endureth to the end shall be saved.*

9) ***BE MEEK:*** Even if you are naturally an arrogant and a proud person, common sense tell you that in time of trial and tribulation, that you should humble yourself and allow the Holy Spirit to take over the prevailing challenges facing you. **Psalms 25:9** *The meek will he guide in judgment: and the meek will he teach his way.* As far as it is the Holy Spirit your best efforts, is His (The Holy Spirit) beginning.

10) ***WALK IN LOVE:*** Exemplify your life like the life of Job. Job in the midst of great destruction said "Though he slay

me, yet will I trust in him: but I will maintain mine own ways before him". You can lose all but don't lose your covenant LOVE for God and His Kingdom. **Job 23:10** *But he knoweth the way that I take: when he hath tried me, I shall come forth as gold.* Job's victory came as a result of His LOVE for GOD and the Kingdom of GOD.

PRAYER POINTS OVERCOME TRIALS BY THE HELP OF THE HOLY SPIRIT

1) FATHER LORD, DELIVER ME FROM THIS PRESENT TRIAL IN THE NAME OF JESUS.

2) ALMIGHTY FATHER BREAK ME THROUGH OUT OF THIS PRESENT OBSCURITY IN THE NAME OF JESUS.

3) HOLY SPIRIT HELP ME TO OVERCOME THIS TRIAL IN JESUS NAME

4) HOLY SPIRIT SPEAK TO ME IN THE NAME OF JESUS.

5) HOLY SPIRIT MINISTER TO MY SUBCONSCIOUS SPIRIT IN THE NAME OF JESUS.

6) FIRE OF GOD BURN DOWN EVERY MOUNTAIN OF DIFFICULTY IN THE NAME OF JESUS.

7) HOLY GHOST BAPTIZE ME WITH YOUR FIRE IN THE NAME OF JESUS

8) HOLY SPIRIT GO BEFORE ME AND FAVOR ME IN THIS PRESENT CHALLENGE ION THE NAME OF JESUS.

9) SPIRIT OF GOD GRANT ME LIBERTY AND FREEDOM BY THE FIRE OF THE HOLY SPIRIT IN THE NAME OF JESUS.

10) FATHER LORD INTERVENE ON MY BEHALF IN THE NAME OF JESUS

11) ANCIENT OF DAY LIBERATE MY THIS SEASON IN THE NAME OF JESUS

12) IMMORTAL REDEEMER BRING ME HIGHER ABOVE THIS PREVAILING CHANGES

13) LORD GOD TURN THIS PRESENT OBSTACLE IN MY MIRACLE IN THE NAME OF JESUS.

14) FIRE OF GOD BREAK DOWN THESE OBSTACLE FOR ME IN THE NAME OF JESUS.

15) HOLY SPIRIT FAVOR ME IN JESUS NAME

16) HOLY SPIRIT RELEASE ME FROM THIS CHALLENGE IN THE NAME OF JESUS.

17) HOLY SPIRIT BECOME MY COMPANION IN JESUS NAME

18) HOLY SPIRIT REPRESENT ME IN THIS MATTER

19) HOLY SPIRIT ELEVATE ME BEYOND MY OWN IMAGINATION IN THE NAME OF JESUS

20) HOLY SPIRIT, DO NOT ALLOW MY ENEMIES TO TRIUMPH OVER MY LIFE IN THE NAME OF JESUS.

21) FIRE OF GOD PROTECT ME IN THE NAME OF JESUS.

22) FIRE OF GOD DESTROY MY ENEMIES IN THE NAME OF JESUS

23) FIRE OF GOD BUILD A WALL AROUND ME IN THE NAME OF JESUS.

24) FIRE OF GOD EXPOSE MY ENEMIES IN THE NAME OF JESUS

25) FIRE OF GOD PROVE YOURSELF IN THE NAME OF JESUS.

26) HOLY SPIRIT REPRESENT ME IN JESUS NAME.

27) HOLY SPIRIT RELEASE YOUR BOLDNESS INTO MY LIFE.

28) HOLY SPIRIT GRANT ME SIGNS AND WONDERS

29) HOLY SPIRIT MAKE ME A LIVING WONDER IN MY LIFE TIME

30) HOLY SPIRIT TURN MY LIFE AROUND IN THE NAME OF JESUS

31) HOLY SPIRIT I WILL NOT REMAIN AT THIS LEVEL IN THE NAME OF JESUS

32) SPIRIT OF GOD LIFT ME HIGHER IN THE MIGHTY NAME OF JESUS.

33) ANGELS OF GOD MINISTER UNTO ME IN THE NAME OF JESUS

34) HAND OF GOD SEPARATE ME THIS SEASON IN THE NAME OF JESUS

CONCLUSION
Ephesians: 4:30-31

Let no corrupt communication proceed out of your mouth, but that which is good to the use of edifying, that it may minister grace unto the hearers. ***And grieve not the Holy Spirit of God, whereby ye are sealed unto the day of redemption.***

The truth is we must all respect the Holy Spirit by what we say at any time of the day. As long as we speak casually we will definitely become a casualty. Most of us have neglected the person of the Holy Spirit. Realize here with me that even Jesus Christ needed the help of the Holy Spirit. **Acts 10:38** ***How God anointed Jesus of Nazareth with the Holy Ghost and with power: who went about doing good, and healing all that were oppressed of the devil; for God was with him.***

At this point, acknowledge and believe in the person of the Holy Spirit. Although I hate to re-emphasize this, but never take the presence of the Holy Spirit for granted. The Holy Spirit is the Spirit of creation, inspiration, revelation, prophecy, therefore look forward to inspiration and innovative divine ideas from the person of the Holy Spirit.

Without contradiction without the person of the Holy Spirit we are helpless against the wiles and schemes of the devil. *I will not leave you comfortless: I will come to you. But the Comforter, which is the Holy Ghost, whom the Father will send in my name, he shall teach you all things, and bring all things to your remembrance, whatsoever I have said unto you.* Develop the lifestyle to pray constantly, always ask God for the companionship of the Holy Spirit.

Song of Solomon 8:13 *Thou that dwellest in the gardens, the companions hearken to thy voice: cause me to hear it.*

As you conclude in this book, it is time to begin a relationship with the Holy Spirit. Welcome the Holy Spirit every morning and every day of your life. Make him you Best friend forever (BFF).Always carry the consciousness of the presence of the Holy Spirit.

Eccl. 12:13-14

Let us hear the conclusion of the whole matter: Fear God, and keep his commandments: for this is the whole duty of man.

For God shall bring every work into judgment, with every secret thing, whether it be good, or whether it be evil.

All you have read remains a story until they is a quickening transformation inside of your heart. The mysteries of God is provoked only when you FEAR GOD and keep HIS commandments. The Bible says in **Eccl: 12:14**, For God shall bring every work into judgment, with every secret thing, whether it be good, or whether it be evil. If you are a born again Christian; we like to encourage you in your Christian life. If you are not a born again Christian we can help you here receive genuine salvation. **2 Cor. 5:17** *Therefore if any man be in Christ, he is a new creature: old things are passed away; behold, all things are become new. Now repeat this Prayer after me*

Say Lord Jesus, I accept you today, as my Lord and my savior, forgive me of my sins wash me with your blood. Right now, I believe, I am sanctified, I am save, I am free, I am free from the Power of sin to serve the Lord Jesus. Thank you Lord for saving me. Amen. Congratulations: YOU ARE NOW A BORN AGAIN CHRISTIAN

AGAIN I SAY TO YOU, CONGRATULATIONS.

What must I do to determine my divine visitation?

To determine divine visitation you must be born again! The word says as many as received him, to them gave He power to become the sons of God. Even to them that believe on his name.

To qualify for divine visitation do the following sincerely

1) *Acknowledge that you are a sinner and that He died for you.* **Romans 3:23.**

2) *Repent of your sins.* **Acts 3:19, Luke 13:5, 2 Peter 3:9**

3) *Believe in your heart that Jesus died for your sin.* **Romans 10:10**

4) *Confess Jesus as the Lord over your life.* **Romans 10:10, Acts 2:21**

Now repeat this Prayer after me
Say: Lord Jesus, I accept you today, as my Lord and my savior, forgive me of my sins wash me with your blood. Right now, I believe, I am sanctified, I am save, I am free, I am free from the Power of sin to serve the Lord Jesus. Thank you Lord for saving me. Amen. Congratulation: YOU ARE NOW A BORN AGAIN CHRISTIAN
AGAIN I SAY TO YOU CONGRATULATIONS

I adjure you to watch the Spirit of God bear witness with your Spirit confirming His word with signs following. The word says The Spirit itself beareth witness with our spirit, that we are the children of God. Join a Bible believing church or join us on our weekly and Sunday worship services at 343 Sanford Avenue, Newark, New Jersey 07106.

WISDOM KEYS

- Every Productive Society is a society heading to the top

- Millions of Nigerians run away from Nigeria, very few Nigerians stay in Nigeria.

- My decision to return Nigeria is the will of God for my life

- My short coming in America after 18 years, trained me to be wise, to think, reflect and reason appropriately.

- If you train your mind to reason it will train your hands to earn money.

- It is absurd to use the money of the heathen to build the kingdom of the living God.

- Every Ministry reveals its agenda and goal either at the beginning or at the end. Be careful of your life it is your first Ministry.

- The average American mind is conditioned for a continual quest to get new things and (discard the former) and throw away old things.

- When I considered well, my BMW jeep became my initial deposit for the work of the ministry in Nigeria

- Money will never fall from any Treebank, Treasury Department or person. Make up your mind to be independent today.

- Everyone is waiting for you to change your mind until you change your thinking nothing changes around you.

- Multiple academic degrees in other discipline gave me the chance to think, reflect and reason

- What so everyone are thinking and reflecting at the moment reveals you to the time and the now factor

- All events and intents are the product of precise thought processes, accurate reason every event is designed for a designated timeline

- Wisdom is your ability to think, to create and invent. If you can think wise enough you will come out of penury

- The distance between you and success is your creative ability to think reason and reflect accurate.

- Success is the result of hard work, commitment resolve and determination learning from past mistakes and failing.

- If you organize your mind you have organized your life and destiny.

- There is a thin line between success and failure. If you look above and beyond you are on your way to success.

- Wealth is your ability to think, power is your ability to reason and success is your ability to be informed.

- If you can make use of your mind by thinking and reasoning God will make use of your life and destiny.

- Think and Be Great

- Reflect, Reason, think and be great

- Famous people are born of woman

- That you will make it is your intention; that you will survive is your resolve, that you will succeed with changes is your determination, personal efforts and hard work.

- No man was born a failure. Lack of vision is the end product of failure.

- Working with mental patients encourages and aspire me to be a productive observant and dedicated to my assignment.

- Successful people are not magicians, it is the will power combined with hard work, and determination and a resolve to succeed that make them succeed.

- In the unequivocal state of the mind, intention is not a location or a position it is the state of the mind.

- So many people think that they think. The mind is used to think reflect and reason. You will remain blind with your eye open until you can see with your mind by thinking.

- There is no favoritism in accurate and precise calculation

- Although knowledge is power, information is the key and gateway to a great future.

- It will take the hand of God to move the hand of man.

- With the backing of the great wise God, nothing will disconnect you from your inheritance.

- As long as you have wisdom and understanding of God, Satan and evil cannot manipulate your life and destiny.

- You have come this far by yourself judgment and decision you have made in the past, now lean and listen to God for another dimension of greatness.

- Great people are common people it is extra ordinary effort and the price of sacrifice that produces greatness.

- As a mental direct care worker I saw a great pastor and a motivational speaker within myself.

- Menial job does not reduce your self-worth, until you resolve to achieve greatness see greatness in all you do; you will never count in your community.

- The principle of Jesus will solve your gambling and addiction problems

- The man of Jesus will lead you into heaven,

- Everyone have their self-appraisal and what they think about you. Until you discover yourself other opinion about you will alter the real you.

- Supervisors and directors are just a position in the chain of command in a work place. Never allow your supervisor hierarchy to alter your opinion about yourself.

- Everyone can come out of debt if they make up their mind.

- That I am not a decision maker at work does not diminish my contribution to my world.

- Although it appears like it was a poor decision to accept a direct care employment at a psychiatric hospital as I reflect of my nine years of experience, it became apparent that I have learnt and experienced enough for my next assignment.

- Self-encouragement and determination is a resolve of the heart.

- If you are determined to make a difference, and do the things that make a difference you will eventually make a difference.

- Good things do not come easy

- Short cuts will cut your life short.

- Those who look ahead move ahead.

- Life is all about making an impact. In your life time strive to make an impact in your community.

- Make friends and connect with people who are moving ahead of you in life.

- If you can look around well you have come a long way in your life, made a lot of difference and realized a lot of success in life.

- If you are my old friend, hurry up to reach out to me before I become a stranger to you.

- Everything I am blessed with inspirations from God, that change my definition and interpretation of the world around me.

CHAPTER 5 • OVERCOMING TRIALS BY THE HELP OF THE HOLY SPIRIT

- I thought I was stagnant and lonely until I looked around and noticed my children running around and my wife cooking.

- At 40 I resigned my Job to seek the Lord forever.

- My ministry took a drastic rise to the top when the wisdom of God visited me with knowledge and understanding.

- You will be a better person if you understand the characteristics of your personality – your mood swings attitudes and habits.

- It is the seed of love you sow into the heart of a child and a woman that you reap in due time.

- Love is not selfish, love share everything including the concealed secrets of the mind.

- As long as you have a prayer life and a Bible; you will never feel lonely, rejected and idle in the race of life.

- When good friends disconnect from you, let them go, they might have seen something new in a different direction.

- Confidence in yourself and in God is the only way to bring you out of captivity

- Never train a child to waste his/her time.

- The mind is the greatest assets of a great future.

- You walk by common sense run by principles and fly by instruction.

- Those who fly in flight of life fly alone.

- Up in the air you are alone. No one can toll you accept the compass of knowledge and information

- I have seen a tolling vehicle I have seen a tolling ship I have never seen a tolling airplane.

- I exercise my judgment and make a decision every minute of the day.

- Decisions are crucial, critical and vital with reference to your future.

- So many people wish for a great future. You can only work towards a great future.

- Your celebrity status began when you discovered your talent. What are you good at? Work at it with all commitment.

- Prayers will sustain you but the wisdom of God will prosper you.

- When I met Oyedepo, his teachings changed my perspective, but when I met Ibiyeomie; His teaching changed my perception.

- I will be successful in ministry if only I concentrate and focus my energy in the work of the ministry.

- It took the late Dr. Norman Vincent Peale's book to open my mind towards kingdom success.

PRAYER OF SALVATION

I am glad you have read this book all the way from the beginning to this point. All I have said from the beginning will remain a mystery until you commit it into practice.

And before you do so I want you, if you have not given your life to Jesus to do so now. Give your life to Christ. I want you to know the truth! The truth is that Jesus died for your sins and because He died you must be alive and prosperous.

What must I do to determine my divine visitation?

To determine divine visitation you must be born again! The word says as many as received him, to them gave He power to become the sons of God. Even to them that believe on his name.

To qualify for divine visitation do the following sincerely

1) Acknowledge that you are a sinner and that He died for you. **Romans 3:23.**

2) Repent of your sins. **Acts 3:19, Luke 13:5, 2 Peter 3:9**

3) Believe in your heart that Jesus died for your sin. **Romans 10:10**

4) Confess Jesus as the Lord over your life. **Romans 10:10, Acts 2:21**

Now repeat this Prayer after me

Say Lord Jesus, I accept you today, as my Lord and my savior, forgive me of my sins wash me with your blood. Right now, I believe, I am sanctified, I am save, I am free, I am free from the Power of sin to serve the Lord Jesus. Thank you Lord for saving me. Amen. Congratulation: YOU ARE NOW A BORN AGAIN CHRISTIAN

AGAIN I SAY TO YOU CONGRATULATIONS

I adjure you to watch the Spirit of God bear witness with your Spirit confirming His word with signs following. The word says The Spirit itself beareth witness with our spirit, that we are the children of God.

MIRACLE CARE OUTREACH

"...But that the members should have the same care one for another"
1 Cor. 12:25

We are all members of the body of Christ. Jesus commanded us to love our neighbor as ourselves. This includes caring for one another as a member of one body. True love is expressed in caring and giving. The word says for God so Love He gave....

Reach out to someone in need of Jesus, help someone in crisis find Christ. Look out and prove your love to Jesus by caring and inviting your friends and associates to find Jesus the Healer.

Invite your friends to our Home Care Cell Fellowship (Miracle chapel Intl. Satellite fellowship).

In the USA at
33 Schley Street, Newark, New Jersey 07112.
If you are in Nigeria—
MIRACLE OF GOD MINISTRIES
A.K.A. *"MIRACLE CHAPEL INTL."*
Mpama–Egbu-Owerri Imo state Nigeria.

(Home Care Cell fellowship Group).
We meet every Tuesday at 6:00 pm–7:00 pm.

LIFE IS NOT ALL ABOUT DURATION BUT ITS ALL ABOUT DONATION

What does the above statement mean?....

Life consists not in accumulation of material wealth. **Luke 12:15**. But it's all about liberality—meaning, what you can give and share with others. **Proverbs 11:25**. When you live for others—You live forever, because you out-live your generation by the legacy you leave behind after you depart into glory to be with the Lord. But when you live to yourself—you are reduced to self—you are easily forgotten when you die and depart in glory. Permit me to admonish you today to live your life to be a blessing to a soul connected to you today. I want you to know that so many souls are connected and looking up to you, and through you so many souls will be saved and rescued from destruction. Will you disciple someone today to find Jesus Christ?

As a genuine Christian; it is your duty to evangelize Jesus Christ to all you meet on your way. Jesus is still in the healing business—Jesus is still doing miracles from time of old to now. Therefore tell someone about Jesus Christ today, disciple and bring them to Church. **John 1:45** Philip findeth Nathanael....

Please to prove the sincerity of your love for God today; please become a soul winner. The dignity of your Christianity is hidden in your boldness to proclaim and evangelize Jesus Christ to all you meet on your way. There is a question mark on the integrity of your Christianity until you become a life soul winner. Invite someone to join us worship the Lord Jesus this coming Sunday. Amen

MIRACLE OF GOD MINISTRIES

PILLARS OF THE COMMISSION

We Believe Preach and Practice the following

1) We believe and preach Salvation to every living human being

2) We believe and preach Repentance and forgiveness of sins

3) We believe and preach the baptism of the Holy Spirit and Spiritual gifts

4) We believe and teach the Prosperity

5) We believe and preach Divine Healing and Miracles (Signs &Wonder)

6) We believe and preach Faith

7) We believe and Proclaim the Power of God (Supernatural)

8) We believe and Proclaim Praise& Worship to God

9) We believe and preach Wisdom

10) We believe and preach Holiness (Consecration)

11) We believe and preach Vision

12) We believe and teach the Word of God

13) We believe and teach Success

14) We believe and practice Prayer

15) We believe and teach Deliverance

This 15 stones form the Pillars of Our Commission. Become part of this church family and follow this great move of God.

MY HEART FELT PRAYER FOR YOU

It is my burning desire for God to touch you through one of our teaching books, cod's. It also my personal desire for you encounter God for yourself.

Now let me Pray for you:

O Lord God! I beseech thee, and through personal prayer intercession today that the Holy Spirit will touch this precious soul reading this book and turn their life around. Spirit of God possess this loved one. Lord overcome all dominating controlling forces that has prevailed over their lives. I come against all oppressive though in Jesus Name. Henceforth; I pronounce you free, from manipulation, intimidation and domination of the wicked enemy called the devil. You are free from all satanic harassment and assaults. Amen

TIME TO TURN TO GOD

HAVE YOU EVER ASKED WHY ARE YOU HERE? GOD PLANTED YOU HERE TO BRING TO PASS HIS PLAN COUNSEL AND PLAN OVER YOUR LIFE.

THE BEST OF YOUR PHYSICAL STRENGTH AND EFFORTS IS THE BEGINNING OF GOD'S GRACE.

ETERNITY IS REAL, HEAVEN IS SURE. BECOME INTERESTED IN HEAVENLY RACE AND BOOK YOUR NAME IN THE LAMB BOOK OF LIFE.

EVERYTHING GREAT COMES BY HIS GRACE UPON YOUR LIFE.

THEREFORE, TURN UNTO GOD IN SUPPLICATION, IN THANKSGIVING, AND IN PRAYER, AND GOD WILL TURN IN YOUR FAVOR.

ABOUT THE AUTHOR

Rev. Franklin N. Abazie is the founding and Presiding Pastor of Miracle of God Ministries with headquarters in Newark, New Jersey USA and a branch church in Owerri-Imo State Nigeria. He is following the footsteps of one of his mentors, Oral Roberts (Healing Evangelist) of the blessed memory. The Lord passed Oral Roberts healing mantle two days before he went to be with the Lord at age 91 into the hand of healing evangelist-Rev. Franklin N. Abazie in a vision.

In all his services the Power and Presence of God is present to heal all in his audience. He is an ordained man of God with a Healing Ministry reviving the healing and miracle ministry of Jesus Christ of Nazareth.

Pastor Franklin N. Abazie, is called by God with a unique mandate: *"THE MOMENT IS DUE TO IMPACT YOUR WORLD THROUGH THE REVIVAL OF THE*

HEALING & MIRACLE MINISTRY OF JESUS CHRIST OF NAZARETH
I AM SENDING YOU TO RESTORE HEALTH UNTO THEE AND I WILL HEAL THEE OF THY WOUNDS. SAID THE LORD OF HOST"

He is a gifted ardent Teacher of the word of God who operates also in the office of a Prophet, generating and attracting undeniable signs & wonders, special miracles and healings, with apostolic fireworks of the Holy Ghost. He is the founding and presiding senior Pastor of this fast growing Healing ministry. He has written over 86 inspirational, healing and transforming books covering almost all aspect of divine healing and life. He is happily married and blessed with children.

BOOKS BY REV FRANKLIN N. ABAZIE

1) *The Outcome of Faith*
2) *Understanding the secret of prevailing Prayers*
3) *Commanding Abundance*
4) *Understanding the secret of the man God uses*
5) *Activating my due Season*
6) *Overcoming Divine Verdicts*
7) *The Outcome of Divine Wisdom*
8) *Understanding God's Restoration Mandate*
9) *Walking in the Victory and Authority of the truth*
10) *Gods Covenant Exemption*
11) *Destiny Restoration Pillars*
12) *Provoking Acceptable Praise*
13) *Understanding Divine Judgment*
14) *Activating Angelic Re-enforcement*
15) *Provoking Un-Merited Favor*
16) *The Benefits of the Speaking faith*
17) *Understanding Divine Arrangement*
18) *How to Keep Your Healing*
19) *Understanding the mysteries of the Speaking Faith*
20) *Understanding the mysteries of Prophetic healing*

21) *Operating under the Rules of Creative Healing*
22) *Understanding the joy of Breakthrough*
23) *Understanding the Mystery of Breakthrough*
24) *Understanding Divine Prosperity*
25) *Understanding Divine Healing*
26) *Retaining Your Inheritance*
27) *Overcoming confusing Spirit*
28) *Commanding Angelic Escorts*
29) *Enforcing Your inheritance in Christ Jesus*
30) *Understanding Your Guardian Angels*
31) *Overcoming the Dominion of Sin*
32) *Understanding the Voice of God*
33) *The Outstanding benefits of the Anointing*
34) *The Audacity of the Blood of Jesus*
35) *Walking in the Reality of the Anointing*
36) *Escaping the Nightmare of Poverty*
37) *Understanding Your Harvest Season*
38) *Activating Your Success Buttons*
39) *Overcoming the forces of Darkness*
40) *Overcoming the devices of the devil*
41) *Overcoming Demonic agents*
42) *Overcoming the sorrows of failure*
43) *Rejecting the Sorrows of failure*
44) *Resisting the Sorrows of Poverty*

45) *The Restoring broken Marriages.*
46) *Redeeming Your Days*
47) *The force of Vision*
48) *Overcoming the forces of ignorance*
49) *Understanding the sacrifice of small beginning*
50) *The might of small beginning*
51) *Understanding the mysteries of Prophesy*
52) *Overcoming Dream nightmares*
53) *Breaking the shackles of the curse of the law*
54) *Understanding the Joy of harvest*
55) *Wisdom for Signs & Wonders*
56) *Wisdom for generational Impact*
57) *Wisdom for Marriage Stability*
58) *Understanding the number of your Days*
59) *Enforcing Your Kingdom Rights*
60) *Escaping the traps of immoralities*
61) *Escaping the trap of Poverty*
62) *Accessing Biblical Prosperity*
63) *Accessing True Riches in Christ*
64) *Silencing the Voice of the Accuser*
65) *Overcoming the forces of oppositions*
66) *Quenching the voice of the avenger*
67) *Silencing demonic Prediction & Projection*
68) *Silencing Your Mocker*

69) *Understanding the Power of the Holy Ghost*
70) *Understanding the baptism of Power*
71) *The Mystery of the Blood of Jesus*
72) *Understanding the Mystery of Sanctification*
73) *Understanding the Power of Holiness*
74) *Understanding the forces of Purity & Righteousness*
75) *Activating the Forces of Vengeance*
76) *Appreciating the Mystery of Restoration*
77) *Overcoming the Projection & Prediction of the enemy*
78) *Engaging the mystery of the blood*
79) *Commanding the Power of the Speaking faith*
80) *Uprooting the forces against Your Rising*
81) *Overcoming mere success syndrome*
82) *Understanding Divine Sentence*
83) *Understanding the Mystery of Praise*
84) *Understanding the Author of Faith*
85) *The Mystery of the finisher of faith*
86) *Attracting Supernatural Favor*

MIRACLE OF GOD MINISTRIES
Healing Crusade Outreach in Nigeria

www.ingramcontent.com/pod-product-compliance
Lightning Source LLC
Chambersburg PA
CBHW021444080526
44588CB00009B/674